Random Mid-Night Thoughts

By

A. A. Coad

Copyright © 2022 by – A. A. Coad – All Rights Reserved.

It is not legal to reproduce, duplicate, or transmit any part of this document in either electronic means or printed format. Recording of this publication is strictly prohibited.

Dedication

I dedicate this randomness to my friends and my family, especially to Hanna and Alan, who have and still put up with my insane ramblings.

Acknowledgement

To Singaporeans, Singapore Taxi Drivers, Cats, People and womankind in general for helping me think out loud.

Table of Contents

Dedication ii
Acknowledgement iii
Sexy Songs 1
   Just talking about Bruno Mars 1
One of Those Days 5
SINGAPORE - The Smouldering Pot!! 9
ESCAPE 24
The Lost Ant in Calista's Hair 27
Fifty-Two And Adding Up – Who's Afraid of Old Age? . 29
Courtesy in Singapore 45
Necessity of Wearing A Bra 53
From My Window 56
   The outside world is very colourful 56
How Do You Know When He Loves You 64
Age is Random 71
Smoking 76
Why Dont You Put Heavy Taxes On Alcohol 80
Are You Hearing Me Or Listening To Me??? What?? 83
How To Know When Your Man Is Not In Love With You 87
Materialistic 93
Life is Hard 98
A Simple Thank You to MJ 103
   - Tribute to MJ in poetry - Rest in Peace 103

Modelling 106
Mock Me 113
Loneliness 116
Just……… 120
Post-Modern Proverbs 123

Sexy Songs

Just talking about Bruno Mars...

Some singers just have sex in their voices, and one of them is Bruno Mars. The song with Mark Ronson, "Uptown Funk", is so dirty, I swear he's flirting with your hearing senses. The lyrics, the beat and just the way he sings it, he's outrageously flirting and oooo so daring *"don't believe me just watch"* and then *"hey hey mmmm"*....noooo... stop it!

Then there's the imagery *"**I'm too hot**"* ... I have never seen the music video, but I can just see him moving deliciously and taunting... oh boy...

And when he sings the part: ***Uptown funk you up*** ... there's that rhythm again ... or am I just too imaginative for my own good.

With singers like him, who needs a video? You just need a wild imagination... and off you go into the singularity of the black hole of ecstasy. What a trip.

So I decided to check out another of his songs just to be sure: Locked out of heaven. He's done it again, though to a lesser degree ... this time, he's pleading ... no... Don't beg...

Must admit he's not exactly good looking; well, not, in my opinion, looks more like a cheeky, naughty school boy, but his **<u>voice</u>** has that ... je ne sais quoi ... maybe it's that sort of mellow, not yelling but rhythmic voice ... it's just very soothing yet tantalisingly teasing ...

I first heard Bruno Mars in the "lazy song", a few years ago ... well, maybe more than a few years and the lyrics sat well with me ... and it was there that I heard that mellow voice ... made me feel lazy but the monkeys (in the video) were so irritating! He didn't need them. His voice did it all. I visualised my ideal man being lazy and cute, then I watched the video, and that put me off for some time. My thoughts were that he was just another misguided boy, shame he didn't optimise his voice.

Then I heard, "Just the way you are". I fell back in love with that voice again... sigh ... foreplay at its best... I wondered if my husband of a thousand years would caress me with the lyrics. Every single word would passionately kiss my hearing senses, putting my ears on fire... ever so gently igniting every hearing nerve. I would close my eyes and just let my ears bathe in the sound of his voice and the lyrics...

Are all of his songs sexy?? "That's what I like" certainly answered my question. There he was again, the lyrics and that "come on over" voice. Teasing, taunting and flirting ... oh lord, stop it. Now he's telling me what he likes ... but feels like he's offering himself up too with that little plea in his cry. Oh... "**Strawberry champagne on ice**", "**lucky for you, that's what I like**".... too right, I say.

One day, I heard "It will rain", and for me, the road forked; he sang with sadness, though he was still pleading, it was sad; I began to feel sorry for him and his love life. There were still a few sexy innuendos with the way he breathed "urghhhh" and "arhhh"... but this time not so in your face. Frankly, I didn't quite enjoy this type of song - not for him anyways. He's sold himself to me as a sex pot, and now he's heartbroken... naaaahhhh... I want the cheeky bad boy who flirts shamelessly.

Don't worry; I wasn't totally put off; I'm just waiting for another song that will drive me wild again.

I didn't need to wait long; out of the blue, I found "Gorilla" ... he was banging (ahem... excuse the pun).

I guess I need to travel back home to see my husband of a thousand years ... I'm being choked by my imagination ... when are the hols coming again?????

Sexy Songs

One of Those Days

My eyes were wide open as I sat opposite my client, body erect and stiff. I looked like I was listening intently, which pleased my client no end. I always aim to make an impression. Pay attention; it's the best way to show your respect to your client.

Bless her, she talked some more, and more, and more... and patiently, I sat. I nodded accommodatingly and smiled appropriately, my timing impeccable.

Every so often, I would add a little "yes", followed by a jerky nod. My body facing her, and my eyes focused on her forehead. Yes, yes, so appropriate. I can be good at body language. My back was stiff from being so straight and arched. My feet neatly and elegantly crossed at the ankles.

Perhaps pressed together a little too tightly.

My lovely client pressed on, telling me in detail what her company requirements are and how we have to follow their schedule. And so I keep nodding, smiling and saying the right thing periodically, "of course", "we do our best". Rehearsed words that people who deal with people use daily, with affirmation and conviction. It is our job to be convincing.

It's been an agonising 45 mins now, and the conversation has taken a different trail. She's now talking about her children. How did we get there...? I don't know myself, the conversation just got naturally deviated, and that's ok too. In any other circumstance, I would not have minded at all, but not today. My eyes were really wide by this time, and she told me that I had really big eyes, I smiled weakly at her and thanked her...

Eventually, after 57 1/2 minutes, we said our goodbyes, with me promising something and her promising another.

Calmly, and in a professional manner, I walked out of the office, one assured purposeful step at a time. By now, I am immensely worried that I might not get a taxi quickly.

As I got out of the lift, I walked with the biggest longest strides; even a professional 6ft tall long-distance walker would not have been able to beat me to the taxi stand. Suddenly, I became quite holy as I saw a taxi waiting in the rank ..."Thank you, God!! I believe!!!" heaving a sigh.

Then the taxi driver started to ramble, oh lord (getting holy again), this time, however, I didn't need to pay attention, well, couldn't actually; my mind wandered, and I began to sweat. The air conditioning in the taxi was on, but I was sweating; I guess that's a good thing considering...

We were 5 minutes away from home, and I already had my money ready for the driver and paid him even before he managed to stop. Nearly threw the money at him as I hurried out of his taxi; poor guy. I shouted back, "Keep the change". He must have thought I was a nutter; there was only 10 cents change...

I ran up the stairs faster than the HULK with his hair on fire and hurled myself down on the toilet in one fleeting move ... just in time, phew ... have you ever held your urge to pee for over an hour???

It's not funny ... now I have to figure out what my meeting was all about ... as you may well have guessed, I wasn't paying attention.... sigh...

SINGAPORE - The Smouldering Pot!!

At 5pm in the evening, on a week day, coming up to Chinese New Year. You're (me really) in a mild mood ... content ...and still have errands to run. So off you go, unsuspecting and innocent... or should I say oblivious to the "world" around you.

Tra la la la la ... ah here's a taxi ... smiling at the driver, I tell him where to take me.

"Huh! What ah! You go there now for what??" he barks at him, like a Rottweiler who has just been snubbed by a bitch.

"Why, ahh, friend? Is the traffic bad? Never mind, lah ... I pay you anyway. But I need to go there, lah", I meekly reply, not wanting to upset this fellow or to spoil my evening. Really, what's the point of arguing with a taxi driver, for goodness sake. I reckoned he's just probably had a bad day, and I'm not going to add to it.

"Waaah! You don know haha, Chinese New Year kamming (** this is not a spelling error) ahhh, so mannny karrs, manny peple orrr... haiii yaaa.... so troublesome oorrh." he starts ranting off," where, aaaaa, in Chinatown you go where aaaa ... north brigge load or sout brigge load side ... nikol highway or cte or ecp or what aaaaa!!"

I sat quietly in the back and thanked God that I always sat in the back. Today, I definitely felt safer in the back.

He went on with his monologue, I guess, he just wanted to moan about something, and I must have looked harmless enoughand not lunatic enough to shout back at him, and that's probably why he kept going on.

"Cann nott lah, go cte now, sure busy one! Aiyahhhhh... I go ecp lah ... traffic bad now lah... how you want to go there haaah. You want or not. You want I take you go ecp lah. Wan or not? Huh?"

Frankly, I didn't know if this was a choice or a recommendation or a simple question... I pondered for a short moment, just to make sure he had nothing else to add, then I quickly put in my two penneth: "whichever way you want to go, my friend, all osso no problem lah. Whatever makes you happy, I don't mind lorrr."

"Ok lah, I go nickol highway, you want" he sighs at me and looks at me in a funny way through his rear view mirror, as if he's tired of me or something. If you didn't know better, you would have thought we'd been married for 30 years and that I was his nagging wife.... **shaking my head in complete bafflement**

"Ok ok you go Nichol highway", I confirmed, trying not to show emotion. Usually enjoy talking to taxi drivers, they are a very informative bunch of people, full of opinions and views and they know all the latest news. I get most of the daily news from taxi drivers, with an aside too. To most of my foreign friends,I sing the praises of Singapore taxi drivers: "they're the best in the world, I tell you". Seriously, I do like Singapore taxi drivers; however, every once in a while, one like this one pops up out of the blue, and it really takes you off guard.

The rest of my shopping trip goes off well; no hiccups, as such but for one thing. This is the thing that upsets me the most and has a tendency to make me want to retaliate, though I do practice a lot of self-control.

What is it? You ask. It's rudeness and disregard for others.

As much as 80% of young Singaporeans are downright RUDE!! Some older folk, too, are rude, about 65% of them. Their rudeness shows in crowded spaces and crowded malls, especially amongst the young. They walk around with invincible blindfolds, and on top of that, they're usually talking to their mates, or are on the phone or listening to iPods or whatever, and thus are on another level altogether. No spatial awareness whatsoever! They are quite happy to walk right into you and not bother to apologise. They don't give way, let alone notice you coming unless you are 1cm away from their noses; then they look surprised as if to say: how did you get on my planet.

I have been to Tokyo, New York, London, Paris and Mumbai and no one! I repeat, NO ONE!! Bumps into you absentmindedly. And if they do by chance, they usually apologise profusely. They seem to be able to skirt around you and respect your personal space.

Let me give you just a tiny taster of what happened at one of the lovely shops in Chinatown today. I was standing in front of a display of shelves inside the shop, engrossed in my own thoughts and trying to make a choice, when out of the corner of my eye, I saw a young man and a young lady coming. They headed straight in front of me, well, the young lady did, and her young man decided to stand right next to me. My personal space was invaded, yes, but that's not the issue. The young lady was standing in front of me for goodness sake!! No word of excuse me or pardon from her, NOT even a nod of acknowledgement. What would you do?? Huh??

"Excuse me, would you like to stand there please, then we can both look at the products," I said firmly. Without so much as a by your leave, let alone a look.

No! Nothing from her. No reaction. She did not look at me or say anything; she just moved to the side, goes in front of her boyfriend instead, this time and went on talking away in Chinese. The silly boyfriend gets blocked now.

"Thank you", I venomously say to her... still she ignores me ... I may as well be invincible. Never mind, I think to myself, just get on with it and make your choices and to hell with her. The ignoramus moo!

Yes, yes, I can be very patient. I know.

That was incident 2. Ah, my day is not over yet, friends, there's one more yet. Once I had done all the buying at Chinatown, I headed for another shopping centre; I needed other things too. So I saunter off with what seemed like a hundred large and heavy bags.

Finally, I'm lucky enough to get another taxi. He was probably the brother of the first taxi driver. When I got in and told him where I wanted to go, but he just sat there, not budging. I thought he was going to turf me out, or maybe he was a plastic dummy. What???? is going on today.... they're all so grumpy and weird ... is it because it's Chinese New Year?? Does Chinese New Year have that kind of effect on people?? Why isn't everyone happy and feeling celebrative??? Why so stressy???

Most people will go on holiday soon, and that should be a comforting thought, shouldn't it?

"Traffic bad! You know!" his projectile vomited the words at me...

"Yes, I know", I reply, being cautious but somewhat slightly irked by now.

"You go by nichol highway, ok" I reply quickly "and be careful, got police car behind you," I said to him, as I had noticed a police car pull up behind us, feeling assured now. I guess I was trying to 'warn' him.... hee...

As we drove off, he started grumbling, "see lah, so many cars, Chinese New Year always headache! All roads busy, cannot move" as the taxi moved easily round the traffic. I was bemused but kept my mouth shut and looked out the window. The view was beginning to look more interesting.

"I drop you off that place; sure I don't get customers, this time, ah, always no people at that taxi stand. No business there at this time, you know" he kept on moaning and complaining.

"How to make a living like this, ERP charge lah, don't know what lah, some more no customers, cannot tahan lah" he was probably talking to himself now ... certainly didn't look like he was wanting a discussion or a conversation with me.

So, I kept looking out the window and enjoying the ride in my head.... zzzzzzzz

"SEEE LAH YOU!!" the yell jolted me out of my power nap ... blast it! I thought.

"Eh, my friend, I'm trying to rest lah", I cautioned him.

"You see, that fellow, wan to turn right, never indicate, any old how one!!" he went off in a tangent again...

And I nodded off yet again, really not caring about what he had to say now.

After what seemed like a lifetime or two, we finally got to my destination; the taxi stand was nearly a mile long, with people queuing for taxis.

"Look, my friend, you sure got customer now," I said to him, out of spite, really.

"Yah lah, but later, I drop off don't know where and then cannot find another customer. Always like that one", he found another excuse to moan about ... you know there's just no pleasing some people. He's the eternal pessimist.

Pay him quick and get outta there!

Went to my destination shop, found what I wanted and then some. An hour later. I'm exhausted and ready for going home when it occurred to me that I was hungry. Really hungry. Gotta eat. Gotta eat Now! type of hunger.

As I was making my way towards the taxi stand and

trying to decide what I could eat, I saw a Subway.... mmmmm a nice sandwich ... yes, what a brilliant idea. I want one. As I glanced in, I noticed there was only one person in the queue. Wooo hooo!!! I'm in there fast ... hunger, you see, it needs attending to.

I waited patiently while the only one staff served the customer in front of me. In the meantime, I stood patiently looking at the menu board and dribbling. Did I tell you I was hungry... mmmm... hungry. It must have taken all of 7 minutes to serve the first customer, then the staff member goes and answers the phone... what!! I felt like crying... hungry...

Ok, stay calm, it's ok... patience is a virtue... I persuade myself. Another 2 minutes go by, and there's a queue behind me now, and it is getting longer. That's ok. I'm next anyway, so hey, patience comes easy when you're next in line, right.

A little Chinese girl (from China, not Singapore) comes in from the back of the restaurant, goes straight to the customer behind me, says something to him in Chinese and proceeds to serve him while I look on in absolute shock.

HELLO!! Am I invincible? I'm 5ft 3in, as tall as the guy next to me and twice his size... how can you miss me???Don't you serve women who are not Chinese looking?? Or is it because I'm older?? Maybe you don't serve older people?? What????

Is this sexism, ageism, racialism, fatism, or has it got something to do with my looks???? Am I too ugly for her??? Do I look too fat, maybe??? Maybe she thinks I'm too fat and don't need to eat anything. What??? I'm not short, so there was no excuse to say she couldn't see me... I was at the top of the queue, for God's sake. I begin to hop, hop hop, hop, hop ... slowly I simmer, and my face begins to distort... now I'm becoming ugly, my eyes start to bulge out of their sockets, my breathing starts to get heavy, my left nostril starts to slowly curl upwards whilst the corner of my mouth twists downwards. Seriously this is an ugly, angry face by now. I fight to remain calm and think of yet another excuse for her behaviour, like maybe she fancied the young man behind me, and that's why she went straight for him and ignored me. The little voice in my head is now telling me to shut up and stand up for myself.

As for that young man behind, he was no better either. He quite happily gave her his order; bear in mind, he knows I hadn't been served because the other only staff member was on the phone, and he did see that I hadn't been served.

Why couldn't this English speaking, educated Singaporean young man acknowledge that it was my turn, not his and correct the "waitress" and tell her to serve me first?? Why didn't he do the 'well brought up' thing?? Why didn't he show some manners?? Bring back the courtesy campaign!!! Why didn't he show some self-respect??? He could see that I was ahead of him in the queue, for one thing, and for another, I was the "older" lady (*I have white hair to prove it).????????????????????? Show some bloody respect to your elders, you little chi chak! (cicak or chi chak is a common house lizard found in the Far East).

To that young man, I have one thing to say: "I want to talk to your mother! Is she so busy working she forgot to teach you manners and respect!"

Frankly, at first, I was stunned, too numb to utter words, seriously, flabbergasted. And that's not one of my characteristic features ... oh no. Just then, the other staff member put the phone down and looked at me, then at his colleague, and he asked her if I had been served; she replied with a nonchalant "huh? don know" - followed by a stupid expression, you know the one I mean, with the lips slightly apart, chin dropped, and eyes drooped... like a wrinkly bulldog, except that she was only in her 20s. You've seen that stupido look before. You know what I mean.

So, he looks at me and says: "Can I take your order, ma'am."

"YES, you can! And it should have been me being served first. THAT! **I point at the girl** That thing blatantly ignored me and served the person behind me first! What is this? How rude is she?" I bellowed at them both. People on the fifth floor must have heard that thunderous voice of rage. Don't mess with a hungry woman with white hair.

"I'm sorry", the little teeny staff guy whimpers from behind the counter... hmmmm, he seems to have shrunk...

Meanwhile, the female who dared to ignore me was pretending that she wasn't there... but I can see her ... and I glare hard at her.... my eyes chucking sharp daggers through my now slit eyes ... you're not invincible to me, girly. Hah!

That fellow who was behind dared to turn to me and even ventured a meagre excuse for a smile ... it appeared to be an apology. TOO LATE!! I gave him my best "dirty" look and watched him shrivel and cower. Suddenly there was a gap between me and the queue.... mmmmmm.... do you think I scared them a bit ... hmmmmmm

Yes, I did get my sandwich. For every question, the male staff guy asked, I would bark back my order, "Yes!", "more jalapenos!", "NO Sauce!"... I was on a rampage in my own way... I think they couldn't wait to get me out of the shop.

"GRRRRR!!Woorrf! Grrrrr! Woorf!"

Now, 3 hours later, I feel calmer; I'm fed and watered and rested. And I'm in hysterics about it all. Hahahhahahhaahahah!!!! It's rather funny, really. What an evening, eh. I'll bet a few people will have a restless night tonight ... hee hee ;-)

Hope you enjoyed your day as much as I didn't mine.... ;-) cheerio, and here's hoping you get better service than this.

And remember, a little courtesy goes a long way.... good night ;-)

ESCAPE

I'm back, but for how long?????? ..... The mind is clinging, though barely, but the spirit furiously tearing the chains of hell,...

The bones are weakening, and the flesh is rotting.

The heart is beating in time to underground blasts, bursting cells with each explosion.

Breathing in the hot lava bursts.

Tears of blood stream down tearing at the tender flesh.

Deep inside, the spirit is fighting for it knows instinctively escape is looming closer...

Where is the strength? To escape?

Emotion has ebbed so low,

Fighting but nowhere to go

The warrior fights bravely though pointlessly

The fight is over, but the spirit is not in synch

It pushes the warrior harder

Eyes no longer seeing

Arm ripped away from sockets

Legs hacked from the knee

but the warrior stands still and unmoving

for his unseen spirit is still alive

Clawing

scratching

trying to escape

No one sees the warrior

No one will remember the warrior

he is but one of many

All he has is pain

All he has is warm blood

all he has is his spirit

Bleed warrior Bleed

He is you, and he is me

The Lost Ant in Calista's Hair

It's dark ... no, it's black, utterly and totally black. No sunlight can penetrate the thick shafts of protein. And every shaft is tightly packed to the other ... the poor little ant cannot manoeuvre at all. He struggles as he climbs the gargantuan black shaft; his muscles ache as he heaves his tiny body.

Ants are supposed to be able to carry 10 times their own body weight, but he doesn't quite believe he can even move his own body any further, let alone carry one of those massive shafts.

He's been stuck in this dense black jungle for 2 weeks now and can't see a way out. The poor little creature feels doomed. Occasionally, it pours with rain, but it hasn't helped him to flush out. He tried to hang on to a loose shaft once, but it didn't budge; it kept getting blocked by other shafts.

"Oh woe is me!" he cried. He cried often at his

predicament. Every night, well, he could not tell if it was night; basically, he just slept when he got tired, as he didn't see any light at all.

Poor poor little fellow.

At other times, he tried to climb up on the forklift thing that appeared through the mass of shafts, but without success, the forklift thing would lift out before he could ever get to it ... he just could not climb over the enormous shafts that lay in his way.

There were so many of them, and so tightly packed together too... oh woe is me!!

The little ant has now resigned himself to a slow death as he lay on Calista's hair... the thick jungle mass of her dark black hair...

Fifty-Two And Adding Up – Who's Afraid of Old Age?

When I first turned fifty, I became a little paranoid for the first time in my life. Age had not figured in my life. Never gave it a thought. It was just a number. What the devil was I to worry about? Blahh… I look good, and feel fine, so what's the big issue, right…. Wrong!

Months into the 50th birthday, disaster hit. I had a lung and kidney infection.

Both at the same time, too … I don't do things in halves… it's all or nothing.

I had a fever for 4 days running, was delirious, and talked nonsense for a while, according to my nurse-maid husband.

Poor fellow, he tried to take me to the doctor, but I insisted that I had the flu and that if he pumped me with enough Beechams and Anadins, I would get better eventually.

HUH!!

By the fourth morning, my patient and, by now, quite frantic husband could take no more and disobediently dragged me to the doctors. Admittedly, by that time, I was too weak to object.

At the doctor's, I sat up straight and confidently in front of him and spoke in a calm voice that it was probably some new virus or even my tonsils. When did I become a doctor, you ask? That I should sit there and tell the qualified medical practitioner what was wrong with me. Pompous. Yes. That's me.

Bless him, the doctor sat there and listened patiently with a little knowing smile too. ;-s

I call that good bedside manner. His medical school training has paid off. Good for him.

Besides, I must have fooled the poor doc anyway; as per usual, when you're ill at home, you suddenly feel better when you arrive at the clinic. Sometimes, I think illness is out to get us, you know. Make liars out of us. At home, you feel like you're on your last breath, and by the time you reach the doctor's surgery, hey presto, you feel better. Then you start to feel wimpy and really embarrassed for wasting the doctor's time.

Within minutes, and in mid-sentence, something happened; I was told this (my husband's words):

"Your eyes rolled back into your head exorcist like, and you flopped sideways on the floor. It was quick. So quick. The doctor and I both panicked. It was unexpected. You were talking away one second and gone the next.

The doctor hurried to your limp body and checked your pulse and breathing; he then shouted for his colleague and the nurses. Everyone was in the doctor's office in a flash. They were trying to resuscitate you. Then they tried to put a needle into you for something or another but couldn't find a vein. They all have a go, first one arm, then the other arm but no vein. (Maybe I'm an alien) Concerned, they called for an ambulance, as they thought you were about to die. That came within minutes, and the medics managed to sort you out and haul you off on the ambulance to the nearest hospital."

Wow! Drama!! I was impressed with myself.

I did the Exorcist thing with my eyes rolling backwards... yee haaa....I managed to create havoc in a doctor's surgery... darn it though I wasn't awake to see it. Darn. Darn.

Admittedly I did hear voices while I was "out" – don't know what they were saying, but I felt amused by the panic around me.... Hee hee ;-) but apparently, I was totally out of it. I don't remember collapsing, but I do remember hearing voices around me ... I guess I must have been on the floor at that time. And I certainly don't remember hitting the floor or what that felt like. Don't even remember falling for that matter. Seems to me like I lost some seconds somewhere.

Do you reckon that I lost time when my brain stopped functioning properly? Or maybe when my senses broke down, as it were. Hmmm.... How cool is that?

Apparently, I was taken to ICU, and they did stuff ... I don't really know what... but whatever it was, after a few hours, I was taken to a room on another ward, as I had stabilized.

In the ward, mostly I remember sleeping ... and wanting to go to the toilet at some point ... I had to struggle to get out of bed to get to the toilet ... seemed to take forever ... and I still hadn't managed to even move from the bed; then a nurse came in and took me ... I didn't call for a nurse, she just magically turned up ... which is good ... I needed the help, I must say.

The rest is boring ... its mainly recovering stuff and taking lots of tablets of sorts ... I had to stay in hospital for 4/5 days ... I guess they needed to make sure I was ok before releasing me back into civilization.

Talk about hitting my 50s decade with a bang... didn't I do that with style eh ;-)

Since then, it's been downhill all the way. I've been well all my life, then I hit the number 50, and bang! It all goes to pot. What?? What?? Why aren't we warned about this?

Don't know when but at some point or another, my middle finger, you know, the biggest fattest finger on your hand, that one, it has started to ache on my left hand. What? Is this? Rheumatism? Arthritis? No! Bloody way. I kid myself; it's just a little ache; I probably twisted it somehow. I wasn't totally convinced by my own excuses, really, but…

Anyway, then the back starts to play up if you do something unnatural, not that I am in the habit of doing anything unnatural, mind you. And sometime later, after working non-stop for 10 hours and climbing stairs etc… my knee starts to act up. So I do what any normal person would do … I take it easy for a day … making sure it's a Sunday, of course. But by Monday, it, being the knee, still niggles. And this perseveres for months and months. And it's a mystery why and what made it hurt in the first place. Doctors are mystified after having done blood tests, x-rays and checks. I'm the new mystery … hahahahahaaaa

OH, and let's not forget the weight … once you

reach 50 and are a sedentary type like me; although I prefer desk-bound, which is more true in my case; you suddenly find that you are no longer a cuddly size 14/16 but have somehow ballooned to a size 18/20 almost overnight. But unlike a balloon, you don't bounce gently, but you plonk around heavily ... more like a concrete block.

But let's be honest, after 16 hours of exercising my brain cells, the body does not quite feel motivated to do aught else, really. Some image-conscious 50-something health freak may want to go to the gym or run 10 miles, not me, though. I'm easy to please; I would rather lay on the sofa and exercise my fingers on the remote control. Hey, thinking is hard work, you know.

Seriously, you have no idea how you got to this size either. You haven't changed your eating habits, nor have you increased or decreased your physical activity in any significant measurable way, that is. So it must be the genes. Yes, it has to be the genes. You search for evidence from your family history.

Ahhaaa ... GRANDMA, she was short and fat ...

very fat in fact. And then there's the mother–in–law; she was huge. Oh, hang on, I don't have her genes.

Ok. Let's try again. Ahhaahh, mother, she has thunder thighs and a floppy paunch too. Dad? No, he had skinny legs. But grandma, yes, yes, I have grandma's genes. It's her fault. She gave me the FAT Gene. There you go, one problem solved. At least we know where the fat gene came from now.

All kinds of other things sneakily creep up on you, a little at a time, so you don't notice it. You discover little anomalies, like that bloating double chin, and the disappearance of the line that used to be the divide between your face and your neck. You used to have a definition between the two areas. But no longer. It's now a republic.

And the sunken dark circles under your eyes, which no amount of cream or foundation can erase or conceal. I am now cousin to a giant panda.

Or the deep deep deep lines that circumvent either side of your face from the nose to the mouth. Seems to me that as you get older, your cheeks get heavy and start to sag. I used to have a slim face, and now I have a swollen face with deep gorges to separate my nose from my cheeks. I've created my own "Berlin Wall". Down with segregation!

And the boobs! That's a whole chapter on its own. They are getting bigger but flatter somehow, and they definitely hang like a cow's udders. One word description: SLOPPY

And how come I have a beer belly that starts immediately beneath my boobs when I don't even drink beer, ever! That's not fair – not fair, I tell you.

Talk about boobs… well, my boobs anyway, don't know what yours are like. Mine have never ever met. Yes, you read that right. They don't know each other. Even when I wear a bra, they still can't see each other. They are strangers to each other. Why? Well, one boob points to the left, and the other to the right. So how can they possibly know that the other exists eh. Cleavage??? What's that? Never Ever had one. Talk about having a valley with two mountains on either side … huh! … I have only ever had a landing strip bigger than 2 airport runways running side by side with no mountains in sight. My mountains may as well be in another country. Push up bras don't help either; the bra pushes up the boobs, but they still don't meet. So no, I have never had sexy boobs. Men, even when I was younger, were not attracted to my boobs.

My arms know my boobs well; they keep bumping into them.

My boobs and my belly are the same size: 38D, except that my belly is more generously spread around.

Thank goodness, after a certain age, boobs cease to be sexy. If you're fifty and don't have any wrinkles on your chest, then consider yourself lucky. It could be worst. I will say no more on that subject.

Then there's the water retention, the wind (not the gentle breeze that blows through your hair type either) and constant indigestion (the type that makes the most horrendous sounds that makes everyone turn to glare at you).

The body begins to malfunction – slowly but surely. Oh yessirree.

And it's always a surprise to you. You never seem to anticipate it. One day you're cute, and the next, you're old. HUH??? When did that happen???

If I was a car, I would be thinking about getting a newer model by now and selling this one off to the scrap merchant.

You begin a journey of many little discoveries about your body that you never knew before. You also realize a few home truths about your grandparents that you were mystified about when you were younger, like how come grandma had a moustache and why grandma and grandpa had so much wind. And why they always belched so much. Why they always talked about constitution and eating of greens. And why they always rubbed their knees obsessively.

I can now appreciate why they always talked about their lives when they were younger. Methinks perhaps they miss having younger bodies and the agility and health that came with being younger.

Now I understand why it was so difficult for grandma to bend down. Her big belly blocked the way, preventing her from bending further down.

Also, I think I understand why my father used to grab hold of his paunch and shake it like it was an alien baby. I guess he was trying to shake it off somehow.

And now I really see where my mother-in-law was coming from when she said that "as ye get older, big breasts are a mighty nuisance" and "what would I be without my corset". A square blob. She was a wise woman indeed.

Saying all this, you may think I don't like being older, but I do; I actually do enjoy being older! Yes, I know that sounds weird. But think about it, I can change my lifestyle and get slimmer, eat better to control the downward slide of ill health, and do lots of good things to feel generally better.

So I can overcome some of the physical minuses of old age, though not the wrinkles or dark circles, but that does not matter really; there is always good makeup out there.

You know what the best part of being older is?

Here is my list:

- It's being able to walk slower than the rest of the crowd and really see what's around you, especially when you're on a zebra crossing and the driver is in a hurry. Or on a pedestrian crossing, and the lights have changed. Go on, I dare you to drive into me.
- It's being able to look at a teenager pathetically until they give up your chair for you on the bus or train
- It's being able to mutter to yourself in public, and no one would think of it as being odd
- It's being able to chat up hot young men/women, and they think you're a friendly old person, and chat back to you and even volunteer to carry things for you
- It's being loudly opinionated in public, and

everyone gently tolerating your "accusations" because no one wants to punch an old person in the mouth

- It's being able to fart in public and not feel embarrassed – your logic is that it is a natural biological function, after all. You spent years of your life holding in your wind; it's now time to be loud. Who cares?
- It's being able to pretend to forget people's names – just because you didn't like them and blame it on your age "ooo, I'm sorry, my dear, but my memory isn't what it used to be" – whilst in your deepest mind, you're thinking "biatch."
- It's being able to sit with your legs apart at last, even if you are wearing a skirt … sod it … who's looking anyway… your older age is your license to forgiveness and tolerance from others.
- It's having the freedom to talk loudly in public just for the heck of it and blame it on your hearing or lack thereof.

- It's having the luxury of sitting back while your children, your grandchildren or anyone else's grandchildren (I'm not fussy) fuss around you and serve you with tea and biscuits… oh yeah… that's my favourite thing.
- It's the sweetness of being able to talk for hours without interruption because our young people have been programmed to respect and listen to their elders … for a change, we get to talk and talk and talk and talk to our hearts' content and not be asked to shut up or be called talkative or self-absorbing… yup I like that
- It's the fact that I don't need to colour my hair anymore because now my face and body have caught up. My hair decided to age first and before its time too.
- It's being taken out by younger family members to dinner and not having to pay for your share … oh yah…
- It's the fact that you don't need to follow fashion anymore because half your wardrobe is already back in fashion anyway

- It's the smug feeling that you get when you look at young lovers and think to yourself – "just you wait."
- It's the gratitude you feel when you return a child to its mum when you have made it hyper, knowing full well that it will take the mother an hour to calm her child down again
- It's the almost evil tinge of contentment that you feel when you see your most hated enemy get as old as you, but her wrinkles are deeper and her neck multi-ringed and dry as a raisin past its expiry date. Old age catches up with everyone…. Snigger snigger …

It's having the lusciousness feeling of knowing that you have been there, done that and still survived it all … to tell the tale and bore the hell out of everyone with your stories. Are you bored yet? Hahahahahahahahaaaaaa

Courtesy in Singapore

That's like a contradiction in itself: courtesy in Singapore. I am tempted to utter loudly: HAH!!

The government spends heap loads (at least I think they still do) on teaching people how to be courteous! As if Singaporeans can't learn to be courteous at home, they have to have this as an extracurricular activity at school. Parents don't instil courtesy and consideration at home, let alone from infancy. Oh no! As a matter of fact, it seems that Courtesy is used as a tool, as I have observed; if one likes you, or if you are of higher social standing, or if you are in the company of your parents / friends / colleagues / bosses / people they want to impress (and you fear being smacked on the head or the back of your legs), then courtesy is practised. Otherwise, you can whistle for it. And even then, you won't get it.

Courtesy has to be imposed on the young early so as they may make it an integral part of their lives, and so that they can have adequate social skills, and hopefully so that they can learn to be respectful to others in society. Well, that's what I thought, at least.

When I first went to Europe, at the tender age of 19 years, I was startled at the 'thank you's and variations of it that I received, the polite: please, that rang so often; and coming from Singapore, I thought the people were being pretentious: "aiyah, every two minutes, say "please" or "thank you", no need so formal lah... hai yah!"

Really, all that politeness was a little overwhelming at first. Wasn't quite used to it being used in every circumstance.

As time went on, I took it for granted and began to expect it too, and actually enjoyed the polite exchanges in daily life. I began to appreciate the little courtesies extended to me. Yes, it was ACTUALLY nice to be polite. I soon realised that with the polite niceties came consideration too. Maybe it was psychological, but it seemed to affect the way we behaved toward each other

... it made us that little bit more considerate, somehow, in a small way, but it mattered.

I was away for a long time; 25 years is along time; Singapore became a world-renown modern destination and excelled in all business and professional aspects... it was amazing and made me feel proud to be a Singaporean. Whenever I came home on short trips, I was always too busy shopping, catching up with friends and family, savouring old favourite cuisines, checking out new places, and so on and so forth that I really did not quite realise if Singaporeans had actually progressed in themselves. If the Singaporean mindset had progressed too.

So you can well imagine when I came home to live here for a longer period, it felt like I was wearing high heels on cobbled streets, and everyone else was wearing slippers. They had an easier time, and I was struggling.... the struggle I encountered is, do I maintain my standards and persevere with them or do I lower my standards and just get into a comfortable stance like everyone around me but still look stupid wearing slippers, as only slippers usually do.

You guessed it, I am one of those that love her fancy high heels and will keep them on no matter what.... blisters and corns and all.... so comes my struggle with courtesy in Singapore.

Let me give you just a few real examples to mull over.

Toe blister one: standing on the MRT train for the whole journey of 15 minutes whilst strong, healthy, under 25s sit and pretend not to see you, let alone offer you a seat. Not that I would have taken it, but the offer would have been nice.

Corn One: Hold swinging door (at the shopping centre) open for a person behind you, and not only do you not receive any acknowledgement at all, but you find yourself having to keep the door open whilst another 50 Singaporeans go through, and none thank you or acknowledgement your gesture or even show signs that you are visible. And as you cannot bear to let go of the door, just in case it hits someone (you are considerate after all), you have no alternative but to stand there like some underpaid, unappreciated doorman, feeling quite a shoe! Humiliated, irritated and quite stupid!

Left Heel Blister: Get jostled by Singaporeans, who race at break neck speed to get to the immigration desk; they then see it's packed and proceed to push in front of you in the 'foreign passports' queue. This I had happen to me at the Batam Ferry Terminal as well as the Johore/Singapore immigration point.

Right Heel Blister: Get a fracture on the back of your feet from being rammed by a heavy steel luggage trolley being pushed by the lady who was lining up behind you in the customs queue. As you turn in pain to look at who the enemy was who bombarded you so viciously, she gives you a sheepish: sorry ahhhhh and resumes her conversation with her companion in Chinese. She is totally oblivious to the bloody oozing from the cut at the back of my heel. And to rub salt on my wound, her companion glares at me whilst I 'litter' the floor with my blood. "Keep Singapore Clean".

Corn on little right toe: At a supermarket counter, I am talking to the assistant about my purchase and trying to select an item from behind her; hence I was craning to see and had my hands on the counter. When, out of the blue, oh, I neglected to mention that no one was in the queue until I was interrupted by an acute and loud interjection of: "EXCUZZZE ME!"At the same time, a basket of shopping was plonked mightily right in front of me on the counter. Please bear in mind that I had not completed my transaction yet, not even chosen my purchase! And don't attempt to give him an excuse like: his shopping basket might have been heavy. He could have placed it on the floor whilst he waited his turn. This was a man at least in his late forties, and he knew how to say 'excuse me', so he must have had some kind of courtesy training, right? Wrong!

Underfoot blister: Whilst riding a bus, lovely air-conditioned number, I notice a few ugly quirks. When you get on a bus, you sit near a window or next to the aisle. On Singapore buses, people (all ages, sexes, it doesn't matter) will usually sit next to the aisle. Ah, I hear you muttering; that's so as they can get up from their seat faster when they have to get off. Oh, well and good. But... then the bus gets crowded, and seats are scarce; what do you do to let another person get the seat next to you that is on the inside next to the window. Huh... I hear you muttering again... you say move over... or do you????? People don't move an inch!! Not a millimetre will they move to let someone in to sit by them! Uh uh! NO WAY! Look here, don't tell me otherwise; I have seen this numerous times. So what is the consequence of that non-movement; well, one person sits comfortably on their own, on a two-seater, whilst dozens stand uncomfortably, wobbling and balancing as the bus starts and stops. How polite and courteous is that action?

There are more, and I know a lot of people out there who have experienced a variety of examples of discourtesy and in considerations. But what I would like to know is WHY? Are we experiencing this in Singapore?? Can someone tell me?

Do Singaporeans have to be spoon-fed all the time; even when it comes to being considerate, we have to be taught it at schools. Do parents ever think of teaching their offspring the necessities of social skills, or is it more important to make money. Why do you have to come from a well to do family before you need to learn simple niceties? Why do you have to go overseas to understand the need for politeness? What a shame it is for us that we cannot even extend courtesy to our own kind. How hard is it to be polite? Is it demeaning to express courtesy and consideration to others?

I am so so saddened that courtesy in Singapore is limited to the office or the few elite.

Necessity of Wearing a Bra

The weather's turned from mild wet to a frosty cold. The change was sudden. It has not snowed yet, but it is threatening to in no uncertain terms.

I wasn't quite prepared for this change in temperatures, though, when I stepped out for a quick fag, one deceivingly bright morning. I slipped on my fluffy house shoes and stepped out onto the balcony to join my hero, who was already outside puffing on his cigar.

"How beautiful it is this morning", I beamed lovingly at him. All I got in response was raised eyebrows. A man of few words is my hero.

I lit my cigarette and took a puff, and slowly exhaled into the atmosphere, feeling somewhat grateful for my pleasant life and this lovely day. Yes, I get like that some days. Irritating, I know, but I just can't help myself.

Just then, without warning, a gust blew from the left (west). It was icy cold. The kind that would freeze water in an instant. And me, without so much as a cardigan on me. "Arrrrggghhhhhh", I shivered, "AAAAffffffffffgggghhhh."
No words could I utter, just these strange muffled sounds "aaaaaaffffgggghhhh".

I tucked my neck down and raised my shoulders automatically like you do. A natural reaction, really. My stomach muscles tensed up, and I looked down to hide my face from that ghastly gust of iciness and what did I see? ...

My nipples ... standing at attention as if in salute to the freezing wind ...

No, you guessed it, I was NOT wearing a bra. Yes, it is a natural reaction for my body.

But what the ... "STANDHUT" ...

Normally, this part of my body does absolutely NOTHING! They are two lazy pimples that do nothing! In fact, I never thought they would actually be this attentive ... ever!

You can just imagine my shock. I glared at them in utter disbelief for a few seconds.

My charming man of few words must have sensed my silent shock, for he turned to look at me and then bemusedly uttered, "You're not wearing a bra... tsk tsk."

The postman who was delivering letters on the street below must have heard us; he turned to look up in the direction of our balcony (we are only one floor up).

Well, quick as a flash, I cover up myself with my arms, tucking my hands snugly under my armpits hugging myself tightly in an attempt to subdue my soldiers back into their sleep mode again. And I give the postie one of my "whatcha looking at" glances forcing him to turn away, embarrassed.

I guess it's time to get the thermals out and start layering clothes and wearing my bra when I step out, eh.

From My Window...

The outside world is very colourful.

I love standing outside my little cottage, puffing on my cancer stick, in the fresh air, with temperatures of 3 degrees Celcius and a gale gust freezing my fingers off as I hang on defiantly to my suicide stick. As it blows icily on my naked face... I sigh... ahhhh.... bliss... shivering and shaking...

Now, now, it is bliss, indeed it is for the fact that after 3 hours, I can finally come out for a quick puff of my "fag"... yes, what else did you think the "ahhh... bliss" was about... its flipping cold out you know...

As I exhaled out, I observed the smoke exude from my mouth and thought, "wow, I am certainly getting a lot of smoke out". I wonder if English cigarettes produce more smoke? Hmmm... I thought to myself. And still, the smoke kept coming out of my mouth ... "wow, I'm impressed with these English cigarettes," I smiled to myself.

Yes, you can stop smiling now.

Duh, it took a whole 1/2 minute for me to figure it out ... duhhhh... I had, for a moment, forgotten it was mid-winter, ok, and elementary science should have kicked in at this point, but maybe I was having a brain freeze.

Maybe it would be cheaper if I just stood outside and breathed in and out ... "smoke" will still come out of my mouth ... do you think I could trick myself into thinking I'm actually smoking... would that work? hmmmm...

So unlike when I was in Singapore when I would take sanctuary in my room and in the cool air conditioning, here, I would need to get my air conditioning outside as it's very warm inside, and we are not allowed to smoke inside. New ruling from my other half. It really doesn't matter, as I still get to see the world go by, and I am still in the cool... though perhaps I should say cold!

I still manage to observe interesting goings-on

around me. ;-)

Like the guy who zooms past me every morning, in his fluffy animal hat ... it's the "in" thing this winter... it looks like a dead furry animal decided to die on your head ... seriously NOT CUTE! but the wearers think it's neat, so lots of people are walking around smug and thinking that they are fashion innovators with this scary animal "hat" on their heads. Seriously, I cannot take such people seriously... picture this scenario:

Receptionist: you're here for a job interview?

We're hiring bunny wunnies right now.

*you won't make it to the interviewer's room with that hat, let alone get past the receptionist. She's the front line for the staff inside the office – no mad people can go past her.

Anyway, back to my story ... go back a few lines, and remind yourself, eh ...

This guy has the skinniest, flattest butt of all time, and as he speeds down past me, he's swinging his tooshh to the left, to the right, full swing ahoy!... seriously campy ... I'm tempted to tell him, he needs some meat on that toosshh if he aims to attract any kind of attention. An unpadded toosshh just doesn't do it.

To top it up, he wears a haughty look on his face, too, as he struts past ... Naomi Campbell, on a good day, would not be able to pull this look off ... I'm telling ya... I have this urge to run behind him and slap his skinny toosshh. But I am afraid that if I do that, I might hurt myself on his skeleton.

Then there are the cats, a whole range of them, roam our street. And these cats are not cat size, no no no... they are dog size!! OK, little dogs but geeezz... they're big muscular and fluffy things and like the young man, they strut too... I wonder if there's something in the air ... hmmm...

They take to the pavements as if it's a catwalk... errr... runway... oh lord... that's it. I stop here... you figure what

I'm saying now and imagine what these cats are like.

One black furry monster came round the other evening and mewed outside our door till we opened the door to it. It just stood there, stared at me and then walked away. Just like that. Err... what??

Did the black cat know we were the newbies on the street and wanted to see who we were??? err...

Then another cat, one afternoon, came round from the top of the road; it was beautiful, long-haired, blue, white and grey coloured... what a beauty it was, and ginormous too.

It stood in front of me and just stared. Of course, I tried to talk to it; it was beautiful; I just had to talk to it. Well, it watched me with an amused look, tilting its head to the left, then to the right, then abruptly, it STRUTTED away back to where it had come from, leaving me feeling most dejected. Couldn't she (too pretty to be a "he", or it could have been a pretty gay boy;-)) hahahahaaaa.... couldn't she have at least come close enough for me to tickle or pat it and allow me the luxury of a purr at least. No, the darn thing just struts its plump toosshh off, away from me... and it was a nicer toosshh too ;-) than you know whose.

Other neighbourhood cats have passed me by on the street, too and gave me nonchalant glances from afar. I guess word has gone around the cat community that there's a new lady on the street already. And none seem too interested ... ahhh well, I guess I will get used to it soon enough. It's not so flattering when cats don't pay you any heed, though.

Cats can make you feel so unnecessary to requirements, can't they. But they have made more of an impact than any of our neighbours, mainly because it's winter and you hardly see anyone, except for the skinny campy guppy with no toosshhh ;-)

And yes, I still love cats, even if they behave like doyens and Prima Donnas ... and make you feel like a second class creature because you are not part feline.

How Do You Know When He Loves You

Everyone woman I know on this planet wants to know this.

Let me be your guru, and show you how to read the signs.

1. When you're ill >he takes you to the doctor or goes out to get you medicine from the pharmacist, or the traditional Chinese medicine practitioner, or the bomoh, or the witch doctor - risking either suspicious looks or all knowing sympathetic nods, from the practitioner when he asks for something for period pains.

2. When you're feeling low >he listens to you moaning and behaving like a spoilt brat then goes out and buys you a chocolate bar and a smoothie shake because he thinks it's your favourite thing. Never mind, if you actually fancied a muffin with a double cream latte, accept that he was at least thinking of you and wanted to please you.

3. When you just want to go out without him >he gives you and your bffs a lift and picks all of you at the end of the night... marry him if he waits in the carpark all night

4. When he lets you have a lie in all day, keeps the curtains shut, switches off the phone and then asks if you're rested when you finally get up at noon... > no, he didn't know you had an appointment in the morning, he

really was wanting you to rest. Forgive him ... he is only a man.

5. When you're stressed out at work and confide in him about your clients, he listens intently all the while. But then when he meets your client, he gives him/her a dirty look and is almost rude to them. Never mind that he is only acting in your interest. You shouldn't have told him so much.

6. When it's your non-birthday, he takes you out somewhere special for no reason except to be with you. Never mind that he did not warn you and now you have to cancel your appointment with your friend to go to that concert that you'd been telling him about for the last 6 months. He means well.

7. He calls you every hour on the hour - to see if you're ok - he really does want to know if you're ok. ... Yes, it's obsessive but isn't it better than a guy who doesn't call you at all.

8. He sends you hugs and kisses on FB/Instagram/Twitter/TikTok all the time and makes

remarks on your status, even though he's just sat next to you.... everyone goes: aaahhhhhhh

9. When you don't have any makeup on, he still looks at you lovingly and says that you're gorgeous... and you thought he was mad.

10. When you argue, and you're in the wrong, and he still comes back and hugs you anyway. He's just made you queen ;-) appreciate that he loves you, girl.

11. When he sits through a chic flick, which he absolutely abhors, but he's happy to do so because it

means he can share it with you. Yup yup, he's in love ;-) You're still dating, aren't you?

12. When after many years of marriage or dating, he still goes shopping with you, even though he hates shopping... thank your lucky stars.

13. When you're older with skin not so supple, and hair not so lush, and he is still proud to hold your hand in public; hey, he really really does love you

14. When you're making a donkey of yourself at a party because you've had one too many vodkas, he still thinks you're funny, laughs at your jokes and then takes you home. That's husband material, don't let go ;-)

15. When you gain afew pounds, about 3 sizes bigger, and he makes an out of the blue comment like, you look good from the back, you know .... he's here for life ;-) or he just likes big booty.

16. When you should be exercising but feel lazy, and he comes back with a comment like: "are you ill, babe? or you just don't feel motivated?" .... he's a lover honey

17. When you go out on your own with your girlies, and don't back till 3am, all tipsy and wobbly, he still wants to make love to you ... then mama, why not ... you know he's besotted, even if you smell of cigarettes and whiskey.

18. When you spent all your salary on that designer bag, and now don't have a penny even to take you to work, yet he still gives you money to tide you over till the end of the month and doesn't ask you for it back ... oh ya, that's one good man, and yes, if you didn't know, that does show he cares.

19. If he puts up with your family, cultural differences and even your senile aunt and crazy mates and doesn't complain ... come on, then what do you think? Elementary conclusion here, ladies.

20. Finally, if he tells you that he would like to watch his favourite sport on the telly over the weekend, he's really asking for permission and your blessing... girl, he isn't taking you for granted ... get it... now go get him.

Now, aren't the signs that he loves you obvious?See,

it's easy ;-) You know he loves you; what are you going to do about it ;-)

Age is Random

2am in the morning and what do you think about? What happened today, this week, this month??? Or just some silly things just randomly run through your mind. You can't predict or manage what you want to think about sometimes. It sort of happens.

Some random thoughts come to my mind tonight at 2am. For instance, my age; it's never been an issue till now. As you get older, you come to terms, for instance, with the fact that you can now come up with your own sayings and obscure witticisms (hmmm... is that spelt right). I am serious; when I was younger, I wondered how my teachers and old uncles came up with such clever sayings, and I couldn't. Well, I've gotten to their age now, and I have figured out how come they're so clever. It's called experience; that's what makes you come up with these wonderful sayings.

When you get to that half-century mark, you go into a panic mode; naturally, it's a big number for anyone.

You start to realise that you're getting older. But worst of all, is that you start checking out your friends, wondering who looks older, you or one of them. That's when you get on the likes of Facebook and all those wonderful social networking sites and start looking for old school and work friends. You diligently search them out just to see if they have posted any photos. Has 'the tart from 5B' put on weight at last and what was that handsome Joe who used to sit behind me, what was he called, dang, wonder if he greyed well ... ooo what if he has paunch now ... yuk!!

You know, I'm so guilty of being an addict to the likes of FB; it's almost embarrassing. FB promotes schizophrenia. You start talking in your head; words form in your head as if you're having a real conversation while your fingers type. You make the expressions, too, in your mono conversation, in your head. You imagine how the person/s you're communicating with is saying whatever they wrote.

Schizo, I tell you.

FB is like a hallucinogen; you know you shouldn't do it so much, but one more hit, a teeny one, won't hurt. And if anyone comes into the office and finds you've got FB, you guiltily hide it away, quick as a flash. I've seen bosses get on FB in the middle of a work day.

It's also bad for the economy. You don't need to go out on Saturday nights anymore, don't need to spend oodles at the pub, club or restaurants anymore, just get your drink next to you, and FB away, listen to music and chatter to your heart's delight.

Internet is not the new highway; it's the new cafeteria; better still, it's the new hangout joint.

Woo hoot!!

Listen, if you're not on the net nowadays, you're a nobody. You're not only behind time; you're prehistoric and a lonely one at that.

If you can't find yourself on a search engine, then where are you???

What would you do if you're bored and can't get on the net, FB and the like? I guess you will have to fight boredom another way. How about FIGHT BOREDOM - MAKE FACES AT YOURSELF IN THE MIRROR

Talking about age, I said this is a random note, didn't I? Anyway, when I reached the big 50, I finally learnt the true impact gravity has on the human body. I learn by experiencing. Gravity is real, people; I have a bruised bottom and can't see my feet anymore.

When you get to this mid-life thing, you begin to see mild inconveniences start to occur; this is the sign that you're headed to "old age"; your mind and body are no longer harmonised and in synchrony. Your mind tells you that you can and want to do something, and your body doesn't even bother rebelling, let alone produce any action.

When Iwasyounger, gosh, I never thought I would ever hear myself say those words. The very sound of that sense used to irritate me when I was younger. Sigh. When I was younger. You also start to repeat yourself, and that's irritating too. Anyway, when I was younger,

I wondered what the world would be like in the 21st century. I yearned to see it. Being an avid sci-fi fan and a trekkie, I half expected humans to have visited Mars in the year 2010 and discovered molecular transportation (beam me up, Scottie)... Now that I am here and haveseen it all, can I go back ... it's not that fabulous after all. No Aliens, no robots in the home, no flying cars... lots of fast food, though.

Maybe I'm kidding myself, but I like to believe that I am growing old gracefully. I dress right for my age. I look the part. But good golly, miss molly, inside, I am just the same old young hooligan, rock chick, longing to go out and party and dance the night away till the early hours. It's the mind again; it just will not age gracefully. Thankfully, the body plods along on its own and refuses to give to the mind.

Sigh... so here I am facing age all alone. It's fine, really. It's fine.

Smoking

Smoking Causes Cancer reads every advert on all cigarette packets; yes, I know, no need to bloody remind me. I am not illiterate or stupid! But thanks for telling me. Duh! I am educated, with average intelligence, a fantastic imagination, sufficiently articulated and am wholly aware of the dangers of cigarette/tobacco smoking. Thank you very much, Mr General Surgeon or Surgeon General, and the Ministry of Health for the warning. I will not heed your warning; however, I voluntarily choose to ignore it!!

I appreciate the trouble you have gone through to place nasty and gory pictures on packets of cigarettes, presumably to put us off smoking. It must have cost the tobacco company millions of dollars to do that, and I realise it's because of your insistence.

But really, you need not have gone to all that bother. I will exercise my rights and still carry on smoking. If I die because of smoking, then so be it. Your concern for my health is touching but not necessary. I am a big girl now, and if I choose to die of lung cancer or heart disease, really, it's my choice, not yours.

Look, I am going to die one day anyway; if it's 5 years sooner than expected, then so be it; I've had good innings and besides, in this day and age of stress and pressure, why the devil would I want to live longer anyway. What's more, I don't think I can afford to live longer; the prices of things nowadays and the rising inflation it's enough to frighten anyone to an early grave. And besides, the sooner I go, the better for a younger person to get my job...... don't mind making room for a younger person.

If you say that the government will spend loads of money on people like me due to medical bills, hey, how often do we get free medical attention anyway. We paid into the system enough to qualify for healthcare. And at the same time, we have to pay for health insurance, so how is it costing the government ???

You reckon I may be harming others. OOOO, I'm sorry, can they get out of my way, please... they don't need to be near me after all. Why don't the non-smokers go out into the fresh air? Isn't that what they want in the first place? Let us smokers stay inside the 'den' of trapped smoke and choke ourselves to death... it's our choice after all. Right?! Why designate us to the outdoors? We don't want fresh air! We want dirty smoke !! Keep us in smoky rooms, please.

You increase the price of tobacco and say it's for our own good.... really?... I thought that it was to line your governmental pockets.... you make a lot of many out of us, and you know it. You know it's not easy to quit our habit, and you know that no matter how much you increase the price, we'll still buy our tobacco; you know the habits of an addict..... you know it's a sure-fire way to make money.... so you use it. You can't get to use via the social outcast modes of yesteryear, so try to outcast us in another way. By threatening us with bad health, and bad hygiene. Tsk tsk tsk.... what tactics you display, Mr Wolf!

Some people will totally disapprove of my views here, and that's absolutely fine. We are all entitled to our opinions. I respect your choice, but please respect other people's choices too. Thank you.

Why Don't You Put Heavy Taxes On Alcohol

Are alcoholics socially acceptable? More acceptable than smokers! Are alcoholics harmless?? Are they not abusive to themselves and to others too? Are families, careers and lives not ruined by alcohol?

Yet it is easier and more acceptable to get cheap alcohol than it is to get cigarettes. Why are we being manipulated thus? Why is alcohol and alcoholics not victimised as much as smokers???

Am I missing the point? Why?

Who can answer me?

Is alcohol more healthy than smoking? Why don't alcohol bottles have health warnings?? with gory pictures?? and abused spouses and children?

When was the last time a smoker beat his wife or smacked his kids??? How many smokers walk into the road in a stupor? How many smokers drove their cars dangerously and killed another person. How many tobacco smokers are unaware or without their full faculty whilst smoking???

Ah, the smoker spat some flam in the basin, geez, that's an offence, put him/her in jail for it. Hah! that smoker just coughed labouriously; call the cops! Oh No! that smoker stinks of tobacco; get the stink bomb police on him/her! Look, another smoker just flicked ash all over the carpet; throw him out!!

Look, I can appreciate that some people are bothered by smoke. Fair enough. But this blatant prejudice is totally unjustified. Give us a break!!!

If you must do this to us, then do the same with alcohol. ;-) that will put a few businesses on the red road to bankruptcy.

Personally, I will carry on smoking. It's my pleasure ... I actually enjoy it. And I try not to inconvenience people, but the thing is, people make it inconvenient for me. How selfish of them. I am no pariah! I don't hurt anyone. i don't abuse anyone. I just want to have a smoke at my ease. if you don't like it, move to another table or go to another venue. Just leave me alone.

I am happy .... what's your problem.

have a nice smoky day, people. :-)) puff puff

Are You Hearing Me Or Listening To Me??? What??

Listening describes an intentional activity. When you are listening, you are actively trying to hear something.

In contrast, hearing is something that happens without any intentional effort. You can hear something even when you don't want to hear it and don't try to hear it. Hearing a function of the physical, and listening a function of the mind.

Many a time, we hear, but don't listen. We hear sounds being emitted from someone's mouth, and we think we know what they are saying, but we really listened to what the other person said; why was there a miscommunication? Why did we misunderstand?

Or did we misunderstand? and we are reacting because we really listened and didn't like what we heard. The utterer of the words just assumed that, as usual, no one really pays attention and relieved himself of his feelings, hoping to cause an effect on the listener.

Have I managed to confuse you?

I didn't mean to cause confusion, just to get you to listen ;-)

Have you noticed that many a time, people response to each in non-coherent ways - to find examples, check out social networks on the internet? It may be to do with the fact that many different races and speakers are all trying to communicate with each other in one language medium, and some people don't have a good grasp of that language. It can be quite amusing to see what people are saying to each other and how they respond to each other. On many occasions, I had to laugh to myself; it was that funny. What is remarkable, however, is the patience and forgiving nature of the co-respondent. People make allowances for each other and politely respond, even if they are confused by the less able speaker.

People are wonderful on the whole and very generous, don't you think.

However, there are instances when emotion gets in the way and then listening takes a different path. When we are emotionally wound up about something, and we discuss it with someone, we usually don't hear their words, let alone listen properly. We usually are governed by our own feelings, and we only hear what we want to hear. During such times, we do not listen. It is a shame, for that's how we create more hurt for ourselves and for others.

On the other hand, why is it that we sometimes choose to listen to negativity? Are we masochistic in a small way? When the biatch or ape said that we look fat, why did we choose to listen when it was obviously malicious. Why did we hurt? Or, correctly, why did we allow such vile words to hurt us? Perhaps they had touched a weak spot. And we all certainly have that weak spot, don't we?

But we mustn't let words injure our soul ... they are only words, utterances of different pitches and tones, coming out of another human. That's all.

The human is a wondrous being with weaknesses and strengths, let's build on our strengths and not let our weakness rule.

Do Be aware of what the utterer is saying ... they may just be malicious, or they may have an ulterior motive, but don't misconstrue the words of the well-intentioned souls who mean you no harm. Listen carefully, don't just hear; with listening, you may learn to differentiate the good and well-meaning from the harmful and nasty.

The choice to listen is always ours, no one else's. Listening is a strength; use it wisely, but use it.

Another time, we will talk about the choice of words, if you want to read it, that is ;-)

How to Know When Your Man Is Not In Love with You

Some gals just don't know when it's time to dump the man, or maybe they're afraid to be on their own. Whatever, here are some signs to help you decide if he's the right man for you or not.

Bear in mind that I am not a glutton for punishment and that I am lazy and appreciate a man who appreciates me. Also that I am bossy when it comes to men... it's in my genes, and I can't help that.

Thus, this is a personal opinion, and you should take it as such.

1. When he takes you out on a date and brings his guy friends with him too. So the night ends up with total guy talk and rude insinuations, and lots of gutter language while you sit around in a corner, smiling like the sweet muppet that you are.... dump the man!

2. When he calls you once a month and thinks that's too obsessive.... errrr.... really, and you think that's ok ... girl, you need help.

3. When he sends you dirty jokes and thinks you'll appreciate them.... are you one of the guys??

4. When he thinks you should work for a living, never mind that you want to work anyway; it's the fact that he insists that you work that's wrong.

5. When he thinks that a woman's place is in the home - 24/7/365 - errr.... doing what at home exactly???

6. When he praises you every time you cook but doesn't bother to help with the washing up. Worse still is when he doesn't praise your cooking but expects you to do the cooking on a daily basis.... that's my pet hate!!

7. When he thinks maids are a waste of money and that you both can do without one and then lets you do all the cooking, washing, cleaning ... etc... girl, you have just been demoted to maid!!

8. When he likes going Dutch because he says that he likes women to feel independent ... so you are going out with him, why?????

9. When he tells you to go out to buy more makeup and perfume! Errrr.... confusing message that one ... is he trying to tell you that you look better with makeup or that you're ugly without makeup??? And what's that with the perfume, most men buy you perfume as a gift (though they can't choose the right one), it spells danger if he asks you to go out and get your own - check your b/o please ... talk to a bff ok.

10. When he has to go out every weekend clubbing because he says he has to network but won't take you with him ... girl, what do you think he's up to?

11. When he takes a lot of photos of himself and hardly any of you... methinks he's in love with himself

12. When he buys things for himself and never buys you anything, not even a telephone top-up card ... gosh, he really has you on his mind, huh...

13. When he goes on holidays on his own or with friends and hardly ever goes with you, except when you moan and scream at him, and then it takes him months to find a cheap enough holiday package ... mmmmmmm

14. When you can't remember the last time he bought you a little something for no reason whatsoever... keep thinking ... when??

15. When a man is afraid of his mom or loves his mom too much ... hello lady, you will be the third lamp post ... get out quick

16. When on a date together, you're both too busy texting on your hand phones to other people and haven't said much to each in the last hour... and you thought that was sharing ... I think that spells: N O T H I N G I N C O M M O N

17. When holding hands in public is "embarrassing"... ok mama, take your hand outta that relationship and find a guy who truly is proud to be seen with you.

18. When you suggest going for a stroll, he starts to moan and says he'd rather go out to the Kopitiam or the pub and that you should join him ... message here is: he does not want alone time with you.

19. When you talk about marriage, he says he's too young, you're too young, he wants to have enough money first, he needs job security, he's not ready, children scare him, he likes being a bachelor, his mama says he's not ready, his friends think he's not ready ... the list goes on and on and on ... stop pestering the man and go out in the market and find another fish will you then see if he can handle that ;-)

20. When he talks about marriage, you have panic attacks and start to perspire; you can't imagine being old with him, you wonder if you're missing out on life, you want to change the subject, you can't imagine having his children, you think that he would be domineering and you would lose control of your life ... ahhhhaaa, you have doubts too ... then don't rush into marriage, just play a wait and see game with him. If he waits, then he's

not so bad, but if he can't, then aren't you better off anyway. ;-)

Materialistic

All that you want in life is the simple pleasures but to get that, buddy, you will need to succumb to pressure. Intense Stress! You know the usual sayings; nothing comes easy, life is hard, hard work pays off, blah... blah... All these are enough to put you off for sure. Why can't things be a little less tedious? Less stressful, less ominous? Why? Oh, why?

- Because the sky's so high and you may not get married in July
- Because life's like that
- Because the Matrix does not exist, and you're stuck in this rut
- Because no one knows the real answer
- Because... that's why!!

Sometimes, you lay back and think... I want to be a millionaire ... but why?

- Because you want Manolos, Jimmy Choos, and Versace
- Because you want a Porche, BMW and a Merc
- Because you want a Villa in Spain and a duplex in Vegas
- Because you want a maid, a chauffeur and a personal trainer
- Because you think you know that all this will make you happy
- Because you know you want people to look to you and treat you well
- Because you want to be valued as someone special
- Because you want to feel like you have 'arrived'
- Because you want to be on holiday whenever you want
- Because the world you were born into tells you this is how to think

But is it, though? Is that all there is? Look deep into yourself, my friend. Is it all about possessions? Or is it about showing off and one-upmanship? Or perhaps it's about financial freedom? Is it about not having financial stress? Isitabout being free to live, to breathe, to have food on the table, to be healthy?

What is materialism? What do you want? Do you really want to be materialistic? Frankly, I doubt it. You are not really a materialist in the true sense of the word. You do have a need, and you and I, too, have confused it with materialism somehow.

And then, sanity hits you smack in the heart, and you realise that you are not alone in this world and that you should be doing more to help others ... but frankly, you don't know how to do that either. Yes, you and I give to charities, maybe monthly, maybe periodically, but it never seems to be enough. It's tiring to be socially conscientious. You think if you could have millions, you would donate so much to the needy, but you know that's a bit of a wild dream. Some of you donate your time and effort. Bless you for doing that. It's immensely valuable. But your core, you somehow know that it's just not enough and it won't solve the world's hunger and ….. I can go on and on, but I won't. You know where I'm going with this.

Basically, we don't know how to make ourselves millionaires, and we don't know how to benefit society. Here comes the depression knocking on your door. So what to do???

Your problem is huge. But at least you are now aware. This is your awakening. Now you know who you are, what is what ... and that, my friend, is a start. Now you learn. Now you are born.

It's not just about possession or giving to the needy... no, not at all. It's about YOU! Learning to understand YOU. When you know what you are, who you are and what you really want to do in life. Then you are at the start, a new beginning of your good life - your path to happiness. If that means giving your time to charitable causes and to people in need, then wonderful! Keep going but be happy doing it, and don't expect acknowledgement of any sort. Do it because it makes you happy and makes you feel good inside.

It is only when you are aware that you can be happy. And when you are truly happy, you become, naturally, truly lucky ... that's the secret.

Do not measure your happiness in dollars and cents; measure it in smiles and laughter. You will be surprised, pleasantly surprised.

You are special, know that, love that. And you are loved. And that should be enough for you and me.

;-)

Have a great life

Life is Hard

What? Yah, it is. Real hard. Love, marriage, relationships, friends, parents, siblings, staff, people you hardly know, bills, money, health, just about everything is hard work...

From the minute we wake up, we have to make decisions, what to wear, what's going to happen today, who will I meet, will I do my work well, do I look good, oh my God, a zit! ......

Frankly, some days, I long for an easier life... some days, I don't want to brush my teeth.... don't want to change out of my PJs... Don't wanna read the papers, don't want television, don't want to check emails, social media........... Nothing!

I would be quite content to lie there in my bed with my cat by my side; note, my cat, not my man, sometimes, he can be hard work too...

All my pussycat asks for is a cuddle and a stroke, bless his little cotton socks. What a darling he is... ... he sure knows how to keep me happy ... he doesn't ask for much ... just cuddles and strokes and food and water.... he doesn't care that I look like I've been dragged through thorned bushes and my breathe smells like yesterday's sweaty socks ... he just looks at me with adorable eyes and purrs with delight that I have time to stroke him.... my kitty is a dear sweet thing, and he's so full of love.

But then, guilt sets in, and I have to get up, brush my teeth, wash the sleep from my eyes, wash off the mascara, shower away last night, make coffee, have toast and look alive again.

It's Sunday; can I just resign from life for a day????

Can I forget that I am broke and have a thousand responsibilities...?

Can I, huh, can I ??????

No, I can't ... as much as I want to. I flipping can't forget, and it's a burden.... how did I get this way ... how did any of us get this way.... why and when did we suddenly become responsible for everyone around us.... for people who aren't family but we still care for them...

Can I just go out and hunt for food and feed the whole village?

Do we really need this ... the internet, radio, TV, electricity, running water, flushing toilets, telephones, mobiles, cars, packaged foods, designer clothes, bags, shoes, credit cards, contact lenses, makeup, creams, perfume....................... the list goes on and on and on.....................

Oh, blast it, I hate to say this, but we do need all this, we do really; we've gotten too used to having these luxuries. Life would be harder without all this stuff, and so the vicious circle goes on and on and on.....

Life's pressures to have fun, to look good, to have the right image, oh blast, I am tired just thinking about it all.... but I will have to carry on just like you will have to too.

Wish there was an easier way of having the good things in life without having to suffer and stress out so much.

Why do we have to carry so much ...... on our poor shoulders.... when did our standard of living get so high.....? Why we are so scared of poverty... when did poverty mean not having the internet, makeup, perfume, a car, a house, holidays, mobile, camera...?

It's all to do with where we live maybe.... so I move country and guess what...... it's the same in most countries..... of course, there are exceptions, but believe me, only a few.

So, don't fight it; conform.

I have to conform, but I have no choice, do you??

I don't want to, but I must conform.

That's enough for now; I am too depressed today to write anymore; I am pre-menstrual, so no point making everyone else miserable, too, eh.

Hence, I sign off now. Will come back again and write some more..... I think, maybe… we'll see…

A Simple Thank You to MJ

- Tribute to MJ in poetry - Rest in Peace

Today for you, we mourn

Our hearts shredded and torn

by news of your demise

your parting seemed so unprecise.

Who would have guessed

your departure was so pressed

No warning

No preparing

we were waiting for a comeback

for your new release to shake and crack

the new generation

that does not yet understand your sensation

Like maternal love, your music & sound

nurtured, made our spirits spring bound

the beat made us reel

your rhythmic lyric made us feel

One of a few

that MJ was you

we suspected your sadness

we never assumed madness

we just loved your music

for us it was terrific

if your life had been different

you would not be so iridescent

I'm sorry your life so torturous but it had to be

for without that we would never see

what wonderful sounds you could deliver

for our ears and senses to quiver

Thank you for the innovation

thank you for the motivation

thank you for moving our generation

thank you for giving us our sensation

Modelling

Of all the things to write about... why did I choose this? I suppose because it irritates me the most. I see hordes of young ladies and men who think they are the next big thing to hit the catwalk. They think they are... no one else does, mind you.

I guess I'm sending out some advice here. Remember the proverb: One man's meat is another man's poison; well, bear that in mind next time you potentially look in the mirror, ok. Your mama may think you're beautiful, but no one else will have the same opinion. When a hundred people tell you that you're beautiful in a span of 3 months, then, and only then, do you qualify to be in the book of the beautiful people. Otherwise, you fall in the category of attractive. And there's nothing wrong with that.

Listen here, ladies and some of you guys too; international models (who have made it big) are not always chosen for their "beauty" sometimes; they are actually chosen for the "unique" looks, for example: Alek Walek; and Omahyra Mota; a lot of times, designers prefer their models to be rather plain-looking. Designers do not want their designs to be upstaged by pretty faces. Not usually anyway. Other designers look for that "look" that is edgy or even unusual, that would deliver and complement their designs. Just ponder a while on this, please.

Models are not always pretty. Highly and bold on "complement their designs".

Reality 2: Makeup makes them look good, as well as good makeup artists and hairdressers.

Reality Check 3: Fashion is not about the model and never will be; it's about the clothes and the designer who created the clothes. The harsh reality is: The Model is a walking HANGER!! - Hence why designers and model agencies insist on them being skinny so that they can carry off the clothes. Skinny never made anyone look good. Slim is lovely, but skinny is plain old disgusting!! Unsexy! And sick... hard to appreciate a walking skeleton. Personally, it freaks me out. aaaarrrggghhhhh!

The sad thing is that a lot of models walk around thinking they're hot and gorgeous ... sorry dolls, but only 10% of the populace think that, and they are usually dirty old men, impressionable young teens and insecure people; the rest of us don't buy into your reality.

You don't need a latent talent to be a model, just be stick thin, tall and be able to walk on two legs, and you'll probably make it as a catwalk/runway model ... I say probably because there's a load of competition out there for the same few jobs. Too many models and not enough jobs to go around.

Here's another reality check 4: there are many modelling jobs out there other than the few catwalk ones. Yes, there are! If you are willing to do them, that is. There's commercial modelling using real people models. This is probably the most lucrative type of modelling, and literally, anyone can do this. You don't need to be tall, skinny or 16. Even your grandmother can be a commercial model. TV ads need real people to advertise their products, and that's what they use, real people. Fat people qualify too!!

And thankfully, in the 21st-century, society has now spoken up, and we see models of all sizes, looks, colours etc... even blind models... I absolutely love it. Everyone will be represented, especially on social media. At last, the advertising agencies are waking up and realizing that we love inclusion.

You can be a promoter; usually, models do this or students who need money. Or you can be an usher for events even. Photography model, editorial model, catalogue model, and the list goes on and on and on... you just need a good agent or be a smart cookie and do your research and network well.

Being a model is not easy and does not necessarily guarantee success, if at all. Be prepared to starve or have a second job or a rich boyfriend/girlfriend, whichever is easier for you.

The one thing you shouldn't be is a snob. Don't carry yourself like you're the next "Naomi Campbell / Gigi Haded" ... be more professional and show some respect for yourself, please.

The most successful models got to the top in the first place by being hardworking, devoted, passionate and very professional in the beginning of their careers. The being bitchy bit came later when they already got fame and fortune. Sad but true. But hey, they only got that way when they attained fame, not before! Don't get it the wrong way round.

One of the nicest and very professional models I have met in the Far East was Amber Chia... her attitude was good and professional, and she showed respect, unlike the other nobodies who modelled in the same event. And I will never forget her for her professionalism. The others, I can't even remember their faces, let alone their names but not Amber Chia. Hence, I will mention her name as an example. Now that's fame. She's one smart cookie.

I don't want to put models down; I just want to wake some of them up ... nudge them into the real world ... and some of them behave like real bimbos; it's sad. All an organiser ever asks is for you to remember details and be on time and do your job; it's not much to ask, is it?. Behaving like a prima donna does not endear you to a show organiser and thus guarantees that you won't work with them again; can you afford to do that?

Remember, you may have earned a few hundred dollars doing one show, but he/she has earned a few thousand... feel humbled a bit, huh? You do one show, he/she does dozens... now do you feel humbled? Good organisers have the ear of the client; you don't! Are you awake yet?

Organisers have a profession that can last years, it does not matter if they gain weight or get old, but a model has a short life span, for the same reasons: age and weight... sigh... am I hitting home yet?

Look, all I'm saying is that you need to know and do your work well, and listen to people in the know, humble yourself a little, learn and see how far you go.

Also, you will need alternatives in life; you can't model forever; it won't feed you. You need other skills; go out there and learn another skill - that's your backup.

Has reality sunk in yet??

Mock Me

I dilly-dallied into the kitchen, greeting our big fur ball of a cat as it was gobbling its biscuits; it barely acknowledged my mumbling.

Sighing heavily as I pulled out the chopping board and knife, then looked aimlessly into cupboards before deciding that I should be looking into the fridge.

Onions, check, pak choi, check, tomatoes check; and what else did I need? Oh yes, fresh ginger and chicken.

Everything got placed on the worktop next to the worn-out green chopping board that was crying out to be replaced, but I refuse to because it's not sustainable. I will persevere till it falls apart, which will probably be never as it's made of plastic, 'heavy duty durable, last a lifetime plastic; and as I'm still alive well... you figure it out.

Onions got chopped up first. As I was wiping my tears, I began to cut into the vivid red chillies; I suddenly realized the chillies were indeed truly vivid, with a capital V, "nice", I thought. Did I accidentally turn on the lights again, I wondered. Nope, the lights are off. So why was I being enveloped like this? It was warm and cocooned my very being. I stood stunned for a moment. I stopped with the knife tightly gripped in my hand.

I thought for a moment, the first clue that I'm an over-thinker. It cannot possibly be; I was beginning to wonder if I was going crazy. What time is it? I quickly jerked my head and glanced at the kitchen clock; 4.30pm. This cannot be happening, I told myself in utter disbelief. What do I do now? I'm confused. Maybe a little panicked too. Do I continue cooking and pretend it's not happening? Do I hurriedly run out into the garden? Do I rush out to the hall and grab at the washing basket? What to do? My thoughts were racing like a desperate formula 1 driver without GPS, racing in all directions.

Instead, I slowly, very slowly, turn my head to the huge kitchen window. There it was. In all its glory. Mocking me.

The Sun!

I wanted to let out a frustrated scream at it, "it's ruddy September, and you decide to show your face now, in the late afternoon at that!!"

"Bog off and come back tomorrow; it's too late now!!" "If you worked for me, I would have given you notice by now!"

English summers, not the most reliable season of year.

Loneliness

A persevering dull ache in your head

Persisting, especially in my bed

Singeing, not so briefly,

heavy with an undesirable stench;

Driving, deriving persistently,

sitting like a judge on a bench.

Inhibiting your mind, your soul, your heart.

Haemorrhaging into other parts of your mind

spreading of undesirable illness, part by part.

 Birthing an abnormality of a kind;

to images that you sluggishly cart,

to weight, you cannot unbind.

Loneliness is cold, but in its path of destruction, it's bold

it wrecks you from within

leaving your skin thin

and your spirit marred and in the fold

You no longer stand upright

Loneliness freezes you with fright

Your arms always outstretched

Wanting anything, even if a wretch

Needing to be with anyone

Looking for a companion

The lonely make mistakes

Erroneously taking comfort from fakes.

Later crying out from the failure

of recognising the wicked allure.

And when you try to fill it

with thoughts and images and sounds,

allowing any little distraction to slip

Still, it does not go away; it abounds.

Always there, like a dog's tick.

A deep devouring black mound.

Oh to remedy this malady

To flush it out totally.

Where is the terminator of this loneliness?

What will rid this ache that was gnawing away in your mindless?

Before Loneliness drives one to madness, confusion and suicide.

A harsh dis-ease inside,

from which is hard to hide.

───────────────

Just………

As I looked at you

I wondered why

Why do you make me so angry

Why … just simply … WHY

You look harmless, like you won't harm a fly

But I know you can hurt me

No one else … just me

Do you mean to?

Sometimes I think you do

Sometimes I think you are just stupid

Sometimes you're just callous

Sometimes you're selfish

You say things without thinking of the hurt it will cause

I'm not your friend; I'm supposed to be your life partner

Not someone you can verbally slap around

And call it 'messing with you'

Don't say I'm too sensitive

Even if I am

Just don't

After all these years, you haven't figured out that you can hurt me

You numbskull

You blithering dope

You are my weakness, you know I love and care for you

But you don't seem to show the same to me

Why … just simply … WHY

One day I will just stop caring

Then what?

Just go fly a kite, why don't you.

Finally, before I sign off, I wanted to share this. It made me smile to gather the below "proverbs." It's modern, and I really do not know who wrote or compiled them, but I'm crediting the website I got them from below. Hope you enjoy them as much as I did.

Post-Modern Proverbs

- If you want your dreams to come true, don't oversleep.
- The smallest good deed is better than the grandest intention.
- Of all the things you wear, your expression is the most important.
- The best vitamin for making friends…B1.
- The 10 commandments are not "multiple choice."
- The happiness of your life depends on the quality of your thoughts.
- Minds are like parachutes…they function only when open.
- Ideas won't work unless YOU do.
- One thing you can't recycle is wasted time.
- One who lacks the courage to start has already finished.
- The heaviest thing to carry is a grudge.
- Don't learn safety rules by accident.
- We lie the loudest when we lie to ourselves.

- Jumping to conclusions can be bad exercise.
- A turtle makes progress when it sticks its head out.
- One thing you can give and still keep…is your word.
- A friend walks in when everyone else walks out.
- The pursuit of happiness is the chase of a lifetime!

Author Unknown[1]

---

[1]Post-Modern Proverbs. (2022). Retrieved from: http://www.appleseeds.org/post-mod_proverbs.htm

CPSIA information can be obtained
at www.ICGtesting.com
Printed in the USA
LVHW081912110622
721067LV00012B/300

9 781915 424594